Jeffers

Breakfast – Lunch – Dinner

Stephen Jeffers

Photographs by Connor Tilson

jeffers
J

Dedication

In loving memory of my mum Jeanie Jeffers, who I dearly love and miss.

Acknowledgements

Many thanks:

To my wife and business partner Lisa and our kids, Katie and Bella.

To my dad Tommy Jeffers.

Special thanks to the best food photographer in Ireland, Connor Tilson.
I also enjoyed his philosophies!

To Christine Sloan for all her typing skills and getting me up to speed.

To the back bone and my right hands on this book – without their belief in me and my restaurant this book would have not been possible – the very hard work of Paul Feldstein and the creative writing of his wife Susan of the Feldstein Agency.

To all my staff, past and present, who have worked for me over the years.

To the great design work of Alan McNally and Philip Bell at Page Setup.

And to the many good friends and customers who have been a great support over the years in both my personal life and business.

A big thanks to all those farmers, fishermen, specialist food producers, breweries and too many others to thank in the food industry. Thanks again.

Keep it simple.

Stephen Jeffers

Table of Contents

Jeffers Mission Statement

At Jeffers, we believe in the beauty of simplicity. Think of a beautiful woman, dressed in an elegantly-cut black suit: when you start with perfection, there's no need to 'gild the lily', as they say.

As far as food goes, we believe that when you've got the basics right – making sure you have the very best seasonal ingredients available – you don't need to fuss or over-embellish. In our book, less is definitely more.

Jeffers cuisine is simple, but full of flavour and with a lot of attitude. We always work with the highest quality, freshest ingredients sourced from the best local suppliers and producers. Everything on our menu – in fact, everything which you will find on your table, including our breads, relishes, tapenades, mustards and mayonnaise – are made from scratch on a daily basis from the finest ingredients.

While simplicity is crucial, our food is always innovative and we're certainly not afraid to take a risk and improvise on a theme. As a chef, I get my inspiration from many sources. One of the most important of these is music, and jazz in particular. The kind of music that leaves you room to stray off the beaten track and have your own take on things. And so at Jeffers, we're constantly reinventing ourselves and experimenting with new combinations and flavours.

We've created the restaurant in the same way that I develop a great signature dish – by putting a lot of energy and imagination into getting all of the elements just right. Great food at reasonable prices; a relaxed and friendly, but very professional front-of-house; laid-back but stylish surroundings; good music with a cool 'jazz' vibe: this is what Jeffers is all about.

Introduction by Stephen Jeffers

I suppose the first time is special for us all . . .

I can still remember very clearly when I fell in love with food, the first time I really noticed its flavours and textures and the exciting possibilities of different combinations. It was in the summer of 1981: I was thirteen years old. We were on a family holiday to the States (a first for all of us), visiting my granny's sister, a great-aunt who had married an American and was living in Connecticut at the time.

Before this, food wasn't something I'd not given a lot of thought to. As a youngster growing up in the terraced streets of the East Belfast of the 1970s, I didn't get many opportunities to taste anything very different or remarkable. My mother's home cooking was as good as anyone else's at the time, but the local fare was very plain and the range of possibilities limited.

Suddenly, here we were on holiday in America, surrounded by dozens of relatives we'd never met before, staying in my Auntie Esther's big and as it seemed to us, very lavish house. The first day we arrived, she laid on a feast for us: home-cured corned beefs and pastrami on rye, a stunning variety of freshly baked breads, homemade chutneys, a breathtaking array of salads, and so on. We'd long suspected that Aunt Esther was good at baking, as every year at Christmas she would send us jars of her own delicious home baked cookies – but now we knew she was a truly great cook. She wasn't a professional chef or anything, though I'm convinced that if she'd opened her own restaurant at the time, it would have been packed to capacity every night, and she'd have been up there with the best.

That first trip to America was quite simply a revelation for me. Every day of that fortnight I would wake up with a feeling of nervous excitement – but it wasn't in anticipation of what new sights we might get the chance to see, it was because I couldn't wait to find out what Aunt Esther would come up with for us to eat that day.

That, for me, was it. By the time we returned to Belfast, I knew what I wanted to do with my life: I wanted to be a chef. I've been passionate about food ever since.

What I loved about classic American food – the type in which my Aunt Esther excelled – was the emphasis on fresh, wholesome ingredients, the pride taken in cooking everything from scratch, the combinations of flavours, very new to me at the time of course – and, it has to be said, the sheer generosity of the unstinting portions. This was – and still is – seriously good food. While my cooking has evolved over the years of course because of many other different experiences and influences, my fondness for the food of the US remains. And so it was something of an accolade for me when, many years after that first trip to Connecticut, a researcher from Martha Stewart's cookery show got in touch saying that they wanted to do a spot on my very Irish take on an American classic – my signature Guinness brownies (you'll find the recipe on page 98).

At fourteen years old, I began to bake my own bread. I was working on a milk round every day before school at the time. My shift started at three in the morning and finished at 8am, and whenever I got back to the house, my parents would be leaving for work, so I'd take over the kitchen and experiment with bread making. Bread's a very good place to start if you're serious about cooking: the essence, if you like: the place where it all begins. And for a youngster, there's something almost magical about it too: the way the yeast makes the dough rise in the oven while you watch; the feeling that you've created something special and delicious out of very little.
As soon as I could – at sixteen – I left home to go to catering college in Portrush, where I spent the next three years.

My first experience as a professional chef was a stint in commercial catering on a large scale at Stormont buildings, home of Northern Ireland's parliament. This was a huge learning curve for me, and a challenge, to say the least. We had to service two very distinct dining rooms simultaneously. There was the very formal Members' area, with silver service, linen tablecloths and leather chairs, and then the more casual, 'Strangers' Dining Room (yes, really, that's what they called it!), where the more lowly civil servants, journalists and the like would have their meals. The kitchen was slap-bang in the middle of these two dining areas – on one side we had the members and on the other the strangers. There wasn't much room for manoeuvre if things went wrong! As pastry chef and then second chef, I learned a thing or two about the importance of presentation (for the Members) and getting my skills up to speed, literally, for the Strangers, who were likely to be in a hurry.

The next key time in my career was undoubtedly my time (six years in all) as personal chef to Lindy Guinness (the Marchioness of Dufferin and Ava) who lives in a beautiful stately home on the Clandeboye estate in County Down, which has been the country residence of her family for many generations.

This 'country house' grounding was a fantastic experience for a young chef, and so much of what I learned there continues to shape and influence what I do today. Faced with a variety of different dining scenarios, often on a daily basis, I learned to be extremely versatile and adaptable, while never letting up on the quality of what I was producing.

Sometimes, I would be cooking just for Lindy Guinness herself - breakfast, lunch, afternoon tea and dinner. On other occasions, I would have to prepare a lavish dinner party for 40 people, or then again, a more intimate dinner for 18 guests. An avid supporter of the arts and conservation, a lover of nature and all things spiritual, Lindy Guinness would regularly play hostess to some of the most influential figures from all walks of life at the time. The Dimblebys and the Rothschilds were regular guests, as were prominent local politicians such as Richard Needham, the designer Terence Conran, such showbiz names as Barry Humphries (Dame Edna Everage), Sean Rafferty and even, I can clearly remember, Mick Jagger. Luckily in one sense, I was too young and too cocky to be overly phased by the idea of having to cater for such celebrities, local or otherwise. Although I do remember being slightly apprehensive whenever I got word one day that Albert Roux himself would be coming to dinner that evening.

Lindy was a very generous, if a very exacting employer. Seeing that I was young and hungry to learn, with a lot of energy to spare, she insisted that I try participating in every level of activity on the estate – from felling trees to shadowing the head gardener to going out on the grounds with the gamekeeper.

I learnt an enormous amount from all of this – about food in its raw state, how to produce or source it and how to get it ready for the kitchen. I also learned that I didn't have a natural inclination to wring the necks of guineafowl! But more to the point, I came to understand the importance of having fresh ingredients of the highest possible quality, and that this is where excellence in cooking really begins. Much as I didn't enjoy skinning rabbits, I did value the contact I had with those who produced the ingredients I would be cooking with, and the opportunity to learn everything there is to know about game, vegetables and fruit, dairy and meat.

That's why, since long before fraternising local producers became trendy and to this day, I pride myself on my relationships with my key suppliers. There is Robert Crofts ('Robert the gamekeeper') who works on the Portavoe Estate and brings me pheasant and other game, as well as homemade sausages and burgers; Clements Farm in Carrowdore, who supply me with duck eggs. I get my lamb from Strangford, while Eric Brown brings us fresh langoustines, crab, shrimps and lobster; Tim Morrow from Streamvale Farm in Dundonald supplies our ice-cream. And I still have important links with Clandeboye Estate, who produce exceptional yoghurt for the local area and beyond. You'll find more information about all of these in this book.

Of course I have a social conscience and believe in supporting the local economy – but, to be brutally honest, for me, it's more about ensuring that I source the freshest ingredients of the highest possible quality at all times of the year. Going local's the only way to do that properly.

Another thing I learned from working in a country house environment is never to compromise on the standard of what you produce in the kitchen. I guess I learned this one the hard way. I can still remember vividly to this day the one and only occasion on which I tried to take a shortcut by serving up to my very discerning employer an apple pie I'd been given as a sample from a local bakery for her afternoon tea. Normally, I'd have cooked everything – from breads to soups to relishes to cakes – from scratch using the freshest seasonal fare. I remember being summoned to the drawing room that day and being told in no uncertain terms that I was never to try to pull a swift one like that again.

I realised then of course that you can taste the difference every time between what's the real thing and what's not, and knew that I didn't want anything that came from my kitchen to be anything less than the best. Since then, I insist that everything in our restaurant is cooked from scratch, and from the very finest ingredients. In the pages which follow, you'll find recipes for Jeffers homemade breads, mustard, pickles, chutney and lobster mayonnaise.

I suppose the next big landmark for me career-wise – before we opened Jeffers, that is – was my foray onto the gastropub scene (before there was a gastropub scene in this part of the world) with Grace Neills, a beautiful listed building in Donaghadee, which, having first opened its doors in 1611, is confirmed in the Guinness Book of Records as being Ireland's oldest pub.

As soon as I saw Grace Neills, I knew I wanted to take it on. I bought the restaurant and pub at the age of twenty-eight. Pretty young for such a venture and a financial commitment of that kind, you might say – but the good thing about that was that the pressure was on to make a success of the place from the word go.

As a chef, I love pressure and thrive on new challenges. The other side of this is that if something isn't working, I don't see any point in wasting time and energy unnecessarily: I believe that if a new restaurant isn't up and running and making a healthy profit within the first six months, then it's better to close the doors than risk further loss. Luckily for me, Grace Neills took off as a business almost immediately.

Although I was aware that many of the public might be expecting the type of food that every other pub in the country at the time had on their menus – lasagne, chicken nuggets and bucketloads of chips – I was determined to offer something for the more discerning diner, by serving seabass, lamb shanks and ribeye. Simple cuisine, but with top-quality ingredients – rather along the lines of some of the best Italian home cooking. Luckily (again) from my point of view, it was this good stuff that people seemed to prefer and kept coming back for. Not a chicken nugget in sight!

To me, that time - the mid-nineties – was the golden age of the Northern Irish restaurant scene. With Paul Rankin and Nick Price in Belfast, Michael Deane in Helen's Bay, Robbie Millar in Shanks and myself in Grace Neills, there was a revolution in food happening on a local level. Suddenly Northern Ireland's diners were learning what really good food was all about, getting a taste for it and coming to expect a lot more from a visit to the restaurant. And we were all doing our best to respond to the challenge and encouraging each other to raise the bar ever higher.

I set up Jeffers four years ago now, in 2005. As with Grace Neills, my attitude was that the place had to be working and paying its own way within a few months. Before opening our doors in Bangor, we put a lot of time and energy into trying to get the key elements just right – great food at reasonable prices; laid-back but stylish decor; a relaxed but very professional front-of-house. Family-friendly dining with a sophisticated twist. Fortunately, the mix was a good one, the timing was right, and the public were appreciative. Within the first few weeks of opening, it was clear that Jeffers was going to be a success.

People ask me all the time where I get my ideas for new recipes, and fresh takes on old ones. I suppose I have many sources of inspiration: the early influences in my career which I've mentioned; keeping an eye on what other chefs are doing, particularly the 'big boys' in England; going to good restaurants abroad whenever I go on holiday with Lisa and our two kids. But one of the main things that keeps my creative juices flowing is my other great passion – music.

While food has been my life ever since that first visit to Connecticut, there is no doubt that music has always been another serious obsession of mine. For me anyway, there is so much common ground between the two.

I started playing trumpet when I was about ten years old. My father was an amateur trombone player in a local neighbourhood brass band, and he used to bring me – from the age of six or seven – along with him to rehearsals to watch. It wasn't long of course before I wanted to play too, and as soon as I was good enough, I joined the same brass band.

I quickly realised however that being in a band like that – where you had to play from sheet music and would be in trouble if you didn't keep in sync with everyone else – wasn't really for me. It was too formal and too regimented: you couldn't really be yourself.

Then, at the age of eleven, flicking through the stations on my dad's old portable radio, I discovered jazz. It was sophisticated, it was melodic, and best of all, I realised that this was music where you were allowed to stray off the beaten track, where you had room to be yourself. That's what I love about food too – having the chance to follow a variation on a theme. Being able to experiment and develop my own take on things

I still play the trumpet now and again – much to my family's dismay sometimes! – and I'm a passable jazz trumpet player. Although I'll never follow the professional route as a musician, music still has a very important part in my life. At Grace Neills, we did our utmost to showcase some of the best local musicians in the business, with a live music spot every Friday night. The great Foy Vance was my Friday night man for a while, along with other regulars like Duke Special, Dave Lewis of The Method, Jackie Flavelle, Norman Watson, the late Foggy Little and my friend the trumpet player Linley Hamilton.

To enjoy being in this business, you have to be able to ride out the highs and lows that come with the territory. Every day is a gamble and if you don't enjoy taking risks, having a restaurant is not for you. As well as the financial uncertainty, there's the constant challenge of having to reinvent yourself and your food, often on a daily basis.

Fortunately, much of this is second nature to me. I'm not one for standing still for too long. I positively enjoy keeping things moving, evolving our menus, our style of presentation – and even the decor of the restaurant - as often as possible. I think this is something which our customers continue to appreciate.

I hope that you'll enjoy this book, and that it will give you something of a flavour of Jeffers the restaurant and Jeffers the food. I hope too that you'll have fun recreating some of our signature dishes and my personal favourites in the recipes which follow.

Stephen Jeffers

jeffers
BY THE MARINA
www.jeffersbythemarina.com
TEL: 02891 859555
jeffers

Breakfast

Cinnamon French Toast & Bananas

When we came up with the concept of Jeffers, we wanted the offerings at Jeffers to be special at all times of the day. When you have had our French toast, you'll see where we are coming from.

Serves 4

Ingredients / Cinnamon Toast

4 thick slices of batch loaf
or crusty bread
4 bananas (sliced)
2 free range eggs
160ml milk
0.8g cinnamon powder
Pinch of salt
0.9g vanilla sugar
Maple syrup
Butter

Ingredients / Vanilla Sugar

750g Caster Sugar
2 Vanilla Pods

Method / Cinnamon Toast

Beat together eggs, milk, salt, and cinnamon. Heat a heavy pan and melt butter gently until pale. Place bread in egg mix, then cook on both sides until golden brown. Keep warm on oven tray. Using the same pan, add bananas and vanilla sugar and cook until caramelised. Drizzle on maple syrup and place on the French Toast.

Method / Vanilla Sugar

Put the sugar into an airtight jar. Split the pods and add to the sugar. Close jar.

County Down Boiled Duck Eggs with Toasted Soldiers

To me, duck eggs were never one of those trendy ingredients – people have been eating them for years. In my childhood days, my Uncle Jack used to bring them to the house as a treat for us every now and again.

Uncle Jack was a true original –a working class man from near the Woodstock Road, he would dress himself in the style of an aristocrat, albeit with second hand clothes picked up somewhere locally. He liked nothing better than to go foraging in the markets in Bangor and Newtownards - and then drop into relatives' houses to share all the weird and wonderful things he'd managed to find on his travels – including of course, fantastic duck eggs from the lowlands of County Down.

At Jeffers, we get our fresh, free range duck eggs from Clements Farm in Carrowdore, via Barr's Eggs – they're generally available for around nine months in the year. Duck eggs are different from hens' eggs, because they have a much creamier taste and texture. For this reason, I like to use them in dressings – just the runny yolk on its own works perfectly as a simple but tasty dressing for, say, an asparagus starter. They're great in some main courses as well – for example, chopped through a fish pie to add extra richness to the flavour.

Serves 4

Ingredients

4 large duck eggs
4 slices of thick bread
(cut into thin even sized strips with no crusts.)
100g Irish salted butter

Method

Fill a small pot of water, place in duck eggs and gently bring to boil. Set timer for 3 minutes for soft or 5 minutes for hard and cook. When timer is finished drain off the water.

Toast soldiers (bread) on both sides and butter, then cut into thin even sized strips with no crusts, and serve with Maldon salt.

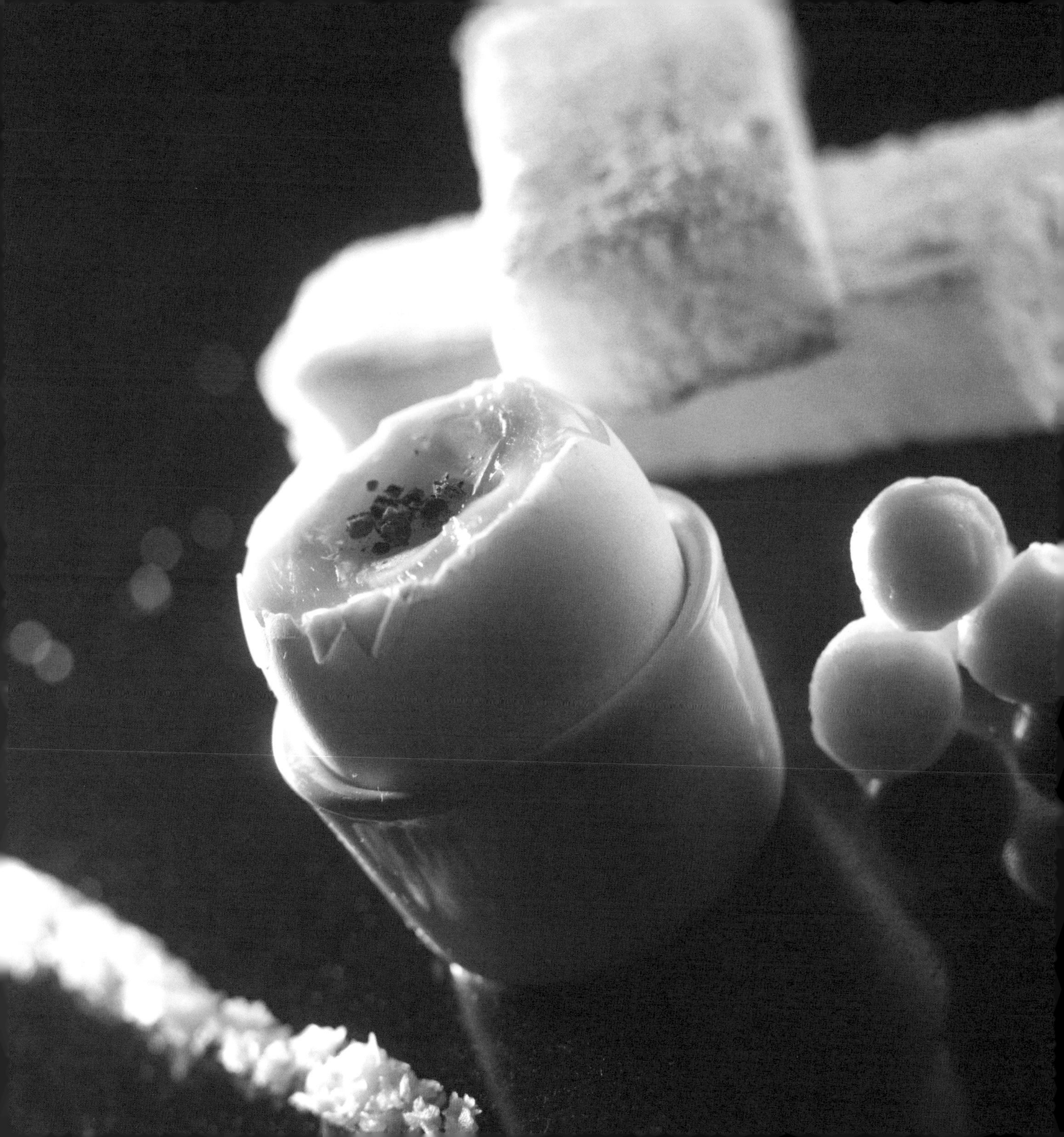

Scrambled Eggs, Smoked Salmon & Toasted Guinness Bread

In true 'gastropub' tradition, I use Guinness in this bread to lend it a rich, malty flavour and moistness. A great alternative to 'the black stuff' here is Molly's Chocolate Stout stout which I get from local suppliers, College Green Brewery in Belfast. The intense, chocolaty flavour of this dark, ruby red stout enhances this bread fantastically.

Serves 4

Ingredients / Scrambled Eggs
8 free range hen's eggs
25ml double cream
Pinch of salt
0.8g black peppercorns milled
2 tbsp Hollandaise sauce
(see page 28)
225g smoked salmon

Guinness Bread / Dry Mix
500g wholemeal flour
120g plain flour
110g porridge oats
2 ½ tsp brown sugar
2 tsp salt
1tsp baking soda

Wet Mix
300ml Guinness
350ml milk
100g butter
75ml maple syrup

Method / Scrambled Eggs
Gently beat eggs, salt and pepper together, then add cream. Gently heat a non-stick pan. Add a knob of butter into the pan and add eggs, stirring with a spoon for 2-3 minutes until fluffy. Add Hollandaise and serve with salmon, toasted Guinness bread and lemon.

Method / Guinness Bread
Place all the dry mix into a large mixing bowl and mix. Put all wet ingredients into a pot and bring to a gentle simmer, do not boil. Now mix into dry mix. Place into a 2lb loaf tin which has been well greased. Cook at 190c for 35 minutes and place on a wire rack to cool.

By adding some Hollandaise and truffle oil to scrambled eggs, you can create a little luxury for breakfast. Also, shaved truffles are fantastic when in season.

Breakfast Mushroom Omelette

Omelettes are so versatile and are great at anytime of the day. This omelette would also be perfect at lunch, served with a truffled rocket and parmesan salad & baby potatoes.

Serves 1

Ingredients

50g butter
100g cooked flat mushrooms, sliced.
2 free range hen's eggs, beaten.
Salt and pepper
Hollandaise sauce (see page 28)
Dash of Truffle oil

Method

In a saucepan cook mushrooms in half of the butter until soft. In a non-stick frying pan, heat butter, then add eggs and mushrooms and truffle oil and cook on a low heat for 4 minutes until golden brown. Top with Hollandaise sauce and place under a grill for 25 seconds.

Porridge with Prunes & Bushmills Whiskey

This Ulster-Scots breakfast dish has a fascinating history. My favourite tale is that in days gone by, leftover porridge would have been poured into a porridge drawer, left to cool, then cut into biscuit shapes to be eaten later that day.

Serves 4-6

Ingredients

900ml full-fat milk
225g porridge oats
1 tbsp brown sugar
1/2 tsp allspice
200ml cream
Pinch of salt
Organic honey
150g Agen prunes
2 tbsp whiskey

Method

Soak prunes in whiskey overnight. Place milk in pot and bring to a boil, then add in oats, sugar, salt and spice. Simmer for about 8 minutes, always stirring. Once cooked add cream and honey to taste, keep warm. Spoon into heated bowls and top with prunes.

Eggs Benedict/Florentine

The famous dish named after the fussy Mrs Legrand Benedict, who was a regular at America's first ever dining room, Delmonico Restaurant, circa 1860. Invented by the genius of Chef Charles Ranhofer, simply because Mrs Benedict didn't like anything on the lunch menu that day.

Serves 4

Ingredients / Eggs

8 free range hen's eggs
4 English muffins (split in half)
8 rashers of smoked bacon
Hollandaise sauce (see below)

Ingredients / Hollandaise sauce

3 egg yolks
0.5ml lemon juice
5ml water
5g salt
2g white pepper
115g butter (diced)
2g grated nutmeg (optional)

Method / Eggs Benedict

Brown bacon under a hot grill until crisp Fill a pot of water 3/4 full, add a dash of vinegar and bring to a boil. Place eggs two at a time into water and simmer for about 2 1/2 minutes, drain with a slotted spoon and keep hot. Place muffins under grill and toast, then place bacon on muffins and top with poached eggs and Hollandaise sauce.
Place under grill for 25 seconds and serve.

For Eggs Florentine

Replace bacon with sautéed spinach, add nutmeg to spinach and sprinkle grated parmesan over Hollandaise and grill for 25 seconds before serving.

Method / Hollandaise sauce

Bring a pot of water to a gentle simmer.

Place egg yolks, water, salt and pepper in a mixing bowl. Gently whisk eggs over a low gentle heat, then start adding butter slowly, whisking at all times. When sauce is formed, add lemon juice and gently whisk again.

Kippers & Mustard Butter

I remember as a child going with my mother to buy kippers on the Belfast's Newtownards Road. At the time, kippers were one of the few fish the average working class family could afford. I've always loved them for their rich, very distinctive flavour.

We have had kippers on the Jeffers menu for a number of years, but this recipe is a very recent addition, inspired by a breakfast I had a few months ago at Bentley's, the Dublin restaurant of Irish chef Richard Corrigan. I was surprised at the idea of combining kippers and mustard, but delighted by the way in which the rich flavours balanced each other out.

I suppose you could say this is a Jeffers' spin on Corrigan's recipe, because we use our own in-house mustard, which is a mild, Dijon-style recipe made with Guinness. It's important to see the good in what other people do, and I'm always looking to get inspiration from other chefs. In that sense, I think we chefs are like magpies at times, taking from the best bits from each other when we need to - although I do always like to give a dish my own spin.

Kippers & Mustard Butter

Kipper is the word for the process in which the common herring is salted, dried in the open air and then smoked. This ancient British tradition dates back to the mid-19th century.

Serves 4

Ingredients / Kippers

4 kippers
4 slices of Guinness Bread
(see page 24)
4 slices mustard butter
(see below)

Ingredients / Mustard Butter

1 tsp white wine vinegar
1 tsp white wine
1 shallot finely diced
2 tsp wholegrain mustard
125g butter
1 tsp chives finely chopped
2 tsp double cream

Method / Mustard Butter

Place vinegar and white wine into a pot with shallots, reduce over high heat by half and pass through a fine sieve. Put all other ingredients in a food processor, add the vinegar, mix and blend until smooth. Scrape out and roll in cling film, and set into the fridge until set.

Grill kippers for 5 minutes, toast Guinness bread, place mustard butter on kippers and serve with lemon wedges.

Bacon Sandwich (see photo page 18)

Serves 1

Ingredients

3 slices of thick sliced bacon
2 thick slices of white bread
Butter
HP sauce

Method

Grill bacon until crisp. Toast bread on both sides, spread with butter and HP sauce and serve.

We use the small, local Central Avenue Bakery here in Bangor for great soda and potato bread.

Granola & Clandeboye Yoghurt

The sublime Clandeboye Yogurt is available from the Clandeboye Estate, as well as from retail food shops throughout Northern Ireland.

Serves 4

Ingredients

2 tbsp vegetable oil
125ml maple syrup
2 tbsp honey
1 tsp vanilla sugar
300g rolled oats
50g sunflower seeds
50g pumpkin seeds
4 tbsp sesame seeds
100g flaked almonds
150g dried mixed berries
50g coconut flakes

Method

Heat oven to 150c Mix oil, maple syrup, honey and sugar in a large bowl. Tip all remaining ingredients, except coconut and dried fruit into the bowl, and mix well.
Tip contents of the bowl onto a non-stick baking sheet and mix in coconut and fruit. Bake in oven for 15 minutes, leave to cool and store in an airtight container. Serve with chilled Clandeboye Greek or natural yoghurt.

The picturesque and historic Clandeboye Estate is of course the home of Lady 'Lindy' Guinness, Marchioness of Dufferin and Ava, for whom I worked as personal chef for a number of years. Recently the Estate has embarked on a new but already very successful venture – the production of Northern Ireland's only locally made cows' milk yoghurt. Clandeboye Estate Yoghurt comprises a range of rich and creamy speciality yoghurts created from the milk of the Estate's award-winning herd of Holstein and Jersey cows. Traditional techniques are used to blend the yoghurts by hand, producing a deliciously rich creamy texture without high fat content. The milk is prepared and cultured very gently in small batches over 24 hours, something which also helps create an exceptional flavour and texture. The yoghurt is currently available in Natural and Greek styles and contains no additives or preservatives – just great natural bounty.

Starters

Crab Cocktail with Avocado & Tomato

This underrated shellfish, the common brown crab, is also simply delicious served with Jeffers' Guinness wheaten, lemon and homemade mayonnaise. Don't forget the glass of champagne... ... heaven.

Serves 4

Ingredients / Crab
500g cooked and picked crab meat
50ml mayonnaise
1 lime (juice only)
Mustard cress for garnish

Ingredients / Avocado Puree
1 avocado, peeled and stoned
1 lime, juice only
1/2 green chilli chopped

Ingredients / Tomato Relish
250g peeled, deseeded and diced tomatoes
1 diced red chilli
120g finely diced red onion
3tbsp fresh lime juice
2tbsp roughly chopped fresh Coriander leaves
Pinch caster sugar
Drizzle of olive oil
Salt & pepper

Method / Crab with Avocado Puree
For the avocado puree: put the avocado and chilli into bowl of a food processor and process until smooth. Season with the lime juice and a pinch of sea salt and freshly ground pepper. Cover and chill. Combine the crabmeat with the mayonnaise in a bowl and season with the lime juice and a pinch of sea salt and freshly ground black pepper.

Method / Tomato Relish
Combine the tomatoes, red onion, chilli, lime juice, coriander leaves and a pinch of caster sugar in a large bowl. Drizzle with a little olive oil and season well. Leave for ten minutes to infuse.

Plating Up
To serve put a spoonful of relish in bottom of glass, then a layer of avocado topped with the crab mayonnaise. Put some cress on top and serve with Guinness wheaten bread and fresh lime.

Tomato Salad

This salad can be changed in so my ways. For example, simply toast some good Italian bread, top with salad, crumbled goat's cheese and toasted pine nuts and you have a very simple, tasty starter. Great flavours!

Serves 4

Ingredients

20 small yellow and red tomatoes (peeled optional)
1 shallot or small red onion
Basil leaves
Oregano leaves
1 small clove garlic
1 ½ teaspoons balsamic vinegar
3 tablespoons good olive oil
Salt and pepper

Method

Slice the tomatoes and lay them out on a large serving bowl. Slice the shallot or onion into thin rings and scatter over. Roll the basil leaves into thin strips, and throw them over the salad with oregano leaves.Immediately before serving, drizzle the olive oil and balsamic vinegar over, and season with salt and plenty of pepper.

Crozier Blue Cheese, Candied Pecan Nuts & Pear Salad

You can use any strong blue cheese in this salad, but at Jeffers we use Crozier blue, developed in 1993 by the J & L Grubb Ltd in Cashel, Co Tipperary. This handmade sheep's cheese stands head and shoulders above other blue cheese.

Serves 4 - 8

Ingredients / Salad
150g mixed salad leaves
150g blue cheese, roughly chopped

Ingredients / Poached Pear
4 pears peeled and cored
150ml water
150ml pear or apple juice
85g caster sugar
1 star anise
1 cinnamon stick
1 tbsp maple syrup

Ingredients / Candied Pecan Nuts
125g pecans
85g caster sugar
¼ teaspoons ground cinnamon
100ml water

Ingredients / Dressing
1 tbsp balsamic vinegar
4 tbsp walnut oil
1 tsp wholegrain mustard
1 tbsp chopped blue cheese

Method / Poached Pear
Place water, juice, sugar and spices in saucepan and bring to a gentle boil. Add pears to syrup and simmer until soft, about 20-25 minutes. Leave to cool in syrup.

Method / Candied Pecan Nuts
Preheat oven to 180 C. Stir together sugar, cinnamon and water in a medium saucepan. Cook over medium-high heat for 8 minutes. Add pecans to sugar syrup, and stir to coat well. Spoon nuts onto greaseproof paper, and dry in oven 5/8 minutes and cool then store in air tight containers.

Plating Up
Mix the leaves, cheese, pears and candied pecan nuts in a bowl. Toss with 4 tablespoons of the dressing, divide between plates and drizzle with the remaining dressing.

Chilled Pea Soup

A great soup which you can make anytime of the year, simply because peas are one of the very few vegetables which freeze perfectly. Can also be served hot.

Serves 4

Ingredients

100g pancetta
2 shallots, diced
2 tbsp olive oil
400g frozen peas
2 tbsp dry white wine
1 litre chicken stock
100g double cream
Sea salt
Ground black Pepper
Dash of Truffle oil

Method

Reserve half the pancetta and chop the rest. Place half the pancetta and shallots in a saucepan with the oil and heat until sizzling.Sweat over a low heat for about 5 minutes. Add the peas and cook for a further 2-3 minutes.

Pour over the wine and cook until it has evaporated.Stir in the stock and cream and bring to a boil. Season and simmer for 15 minutes.Blend and pass through a sieve, then leave to cool and refrigerate. Meanwhile, grill the pancetta until crispy. When the soup is well chilled, check the seasoning and stir in truffle oil and sprinkle with the pancetta.

Goat's Cheese Fritters, Beetroot Vinaigrette & Pickled Walnuts

This Jeffers old favourite was the subject of a review by a local journalist, who referred to it as a cheese style Ferrero Rocher. I never thought of this dish that way but that's journalists for you.

Serves 4

Ingredients / Goat's Cheese
250g of goat's cheese
Small bunch of chives
100g bread crumbs
1 egg
100g plain flour
Salt and pepper

Ingredients / Pickled Walnuts
500g walnuts
50g salt
250ml malt vinegar
125g brown sugar
1/4 tsp all spice
1/4 tsp cloves
1/8 tsp cinnamon
1/4 tbsp grated ginger

Ingredients / Beetroot Vinaigrette
25g peeled beetroot
25g diced beetroot
60ml beetroot juice
25ml port
35ml olive oil
20ml sherry vinegar

Method / Goat's Cheese
Crumble goat's cheese into a small bowl. Chop chives finely, and add to goat's cheese and season. Rub into small balls. Set in fridge for 1 hour. Now add goat's cheese balls to flour, egg wash and bread crumb and chill again for 1 hour.

Method / Pickled Walnuts
Bring the pickling ingredients, excluding walnuts, to the boil and simmer for 15 minutes.Add walnuts for another 10 minutes and put into an airtight jar.

Method / Beetroot Vinaigrette
Reduce port in a hot pan to a syrup. Add beetroot juice and reduce by half. Put remaining ingredients in a blender except diced beetroot, mix, then add port/vinegar and beetroot syrup to form the dressing. Season to taste.

Plating Up
Deep fry for a few seconds, then present and arrange with walnuts, vinaigrette, greens and diced beetroot.

Potted North Atlantic Shrimps with Brown Bread & Lemon

I love these little shrimps when in season. They are so sweet and delicious that we can't get enough of them at Jeffers. Eric the fisherman can confirm this. They are so popular that sometimes we'll even get a delivery twice a day.

Serves 4-6

Ingredients

110g unsalted butter
Pinch of cayenne pepper
Pinch of mace
550g brown or Atlantic shrimps
Juice of 1 lemon.
Watercress
Brown bread

Method

Place butter into pot with pepper and mace and melt slowly, then add shrimps. Stir well, then add lemon juice. Place shrimps into pots or ramekins and press. Top with remaining butter and place in fridge. Serve with watercress, lemon and brown bread.

Potted Duck with Green Peppercorns & Carson Cider Jelly

This modern way to serve the classic French dish duck rillette was our take at Jeffers last year, by default. We wanted to present this dish in a parfait jar, but the jar was too big for the duck on its own, so I came up with the idea to serve it on a cider jelly. It's now a Jeffers classic. Use Carson's cider from Armagh – great local cider.

Serves 4

Ingredients / Potted Duck

4 small female duck legs
150ml Carson cider
1 bay leaf
4 sprigs of thyme,
4 cloves of garlic, crushed
1 pinch of mace
30ml calvados reduced
12 green peppercorns
Cider Jelly (see below)

Ingredients / Cider Jelly

570ml Carson cider
1 cinnamon stick
2 cloves
1 star anise
1 tsp light brown sugar
1 tbsp calvados
4 tsp powdered gelatine

Method / Potted Duck

Season duck legs and place into casserole dish with cider, bay leaf, garlic and thyme. Cook in a very low oven for 2-3 hours until meat is falling off the bone. Drain, sieve and keep cooking liquid. When duck is cool, skin and shred finely. Season with mace, salt, peppercorns and reduced calvados.

Mix a little of cooking liquid with duck and put into pots and leave to set for 6 hours. Serve with cider jelly and a toasted French baguette. You can serve the jelly separate or set it in the parfait jar before you add the duck.

Method / Cider Jelly

Place cider, cinnamon, cloves, star anise and sugar in pot. Gently simmer for 10 minutes to infuse spices. Pass through a fine sieve, then add gelatine and calvados and return to heat. Gently whisk until gelatine is dissolved. Cool and store in jars.

Irish Smoked Eel with Bacon & Duck Egg Salad

Lough Neagh is the biggest lough in the British Isles. They say there is enough water to fill seven million swimming pools! The first time I worked with eel was in Clandeboye estate. Smoked eel was a favourite of my old employer Lindy Guinness. She loved this served simply with watercress and horse radish.......class stuff.

Serves 4

Ingredients
250g smoked eel
4 duck eggs
40g watercress or mustardcress
4 slices of streaky bacon
6 new potatoes

Ingredients / Dressing
2 tbsp creamed horseradish
6 tbsp light olive oil
2 tbsp champagne vinegar
Salt and pepper

Method
Boil duck eggs in salted water, 3 minutes for soft or 5 minutes for hard, then place into iced water and peel. Grill bacon on both sides until crisp, then place onto kitchen paper. Make the vinaigrette by whisking horseradish, oil and vinegar together and season. Cut egg in half, place everything on plate and dress with vinaigrette.

Chicken Liver & Foie Gras Parfait with Fig Jam

Parfait is the posh paté, so much smoother than paté, and a favourite at Jeffers.

Serves 8-10

Ingredients / Chicken Liver

175g chicken liver
125g foie gras
1 egg
50ml port
100ml cream
1 tsp garlic puree
Pink salt if possible

Ingredients / Fig Jam

1.5kg figs
750g jam sugar (with pectin)

Method / Chicken Liver

Place chicken livers into blender and gently blend. Add foie gras, egg, garlic and port. Blend again until smooth. Add cream and salt blend at high speed for a few seconds. Pass through a fine sieve into a plastic jug. Pour into ramekins and cook in water bath at 60c for about 15 minutes, until set. When cool cover with melted butter and set in fridge until cool. Serve with toasted crusty bread and fig jam.

Method / Fig Jam

Cut stems of figs and put into saucepan, squash figs with fork. Put pan onto low heat and add sugar, bring heat up to boil and cook for 4-7 minutes stirring until thick. Then give it a quick blend. Heat jam until 150C. Once cooled put jam into sterilised jars and cover with wax paper & lid. Will keep up to six months.

Serve with toasted sourdough bread.

Crab Cakes with Asian Dressings

The great thing about crab is that it's in season most of the year. I get my crab for the restaurant from Eric Brown. Eric fishes very locally, around the nearby Copeland Islands. He brings me a wonderful selection of the freshest seafood – langoustines, crayfish, North Atlantic shrimp and lobster – straight from the catch. His crab, in particular, is outrageously good, which is why my nickname for him is 'Eric, King of Crabs'.

Serves 4

Ingredients / Crab Cakes

350g crab meat
Small knob of root ginger, peeled and grated.
2 tsp coriander, chopped finely
Squeeze of lime
200g diced white fish
3 tbsp double cream
Zest and juice of 1 lemon
2 egg whites
Salt and pepper

Ingredients / Chilli dressing

Small knob of root ginger, peeled and grated.
4 red chillies, de-seeded
2 garlic cloves, chopped finely
6 tbsp vegetable oil
2 tbsp soy sauce
4 limes

Ingredients / Coriander dressing

4 tbsp chopped coriander
4 tbsp soft brown sugar
2 tsp fish sauce
8 tbsp fresh lime juice
4 cloves of garlic, chopped

Method / Crab Cakes

Lightly mix ginger, coriander and crab meat in a bowl. Place the rest of the ingredients in a food processor and whizz ingredients until coarse. Put this mixture into the bowl with the crab and mix together. With clean, dry hands, shape the mixture into 4 or 8 balls depending on the desired size. Chill in the fridge for two hours. Fry in a non-stick pan for 3-4 minutes on each side. Serve with a small pot each of Lime and Coriander dressing and Chilli dressing.

Method / Chilli dressing

Put ginger, chillies and garlic into a blender and mix. Add the juice of 4 limes, oil and coriander and whisk all together.

Method / Coriander dressing

Place coriander, brown sugar, fish sauce, lime juice and garlic in a small bowl and mix.

'Eric the Fisherman'

Eric Brown from Groomsport supplies me with some of the highest quality and the freshest seafood available in the local area: langoustines, lobster, shrimps and fantastic fresh turbot. But his absolute specialty has got to be his crab – hence my nickname for him: 'Eric, King of Crabs'. The crabs he brings in are doubtless so exceptional because of the vast and richly abundant mussel beds to be found in the areas of Belfast Lough where Eric tends to fish most: between Bangor and Orlock point, or between Kilroot and Blackhead. Crab love to feed on mussels and such high quality nutrients mean that they will quickly grow to their full and flavoursome potential.

Eric has made his living from fishing since 1979, and as far as I'm concerned, he's a fisherman heart and soul. Fishing is such tough, backbreaking and often thankless work, and yet Eric'll go out there in all weathers, regardless. Even the good weather can bring its problems for a fisherman, as the obligatory heavy oilskins will mean that you're often dripping in sweat within no time at all. Passionate about fishing even as a schoolboy, Eric says that he cannot imagine doing anything else.

Ham Hock & Portavoe Estate Game Terrine

I now get a lot of my game directly from the small estate of Portavoe in Donaghadee. Robert the gamekeeper there is a close neighbour, and he'll make a regular delivery of a selection of whatever game is in season. Partridge is available from 12 September every year, wild duck from 20 September, and pheasant from the beginning of October. Robert will have expertly prepared all the game he brings me, including his pheasant sausages, which are second to none!

Serves 8-10

Ingredients

2 ham hocks
1 pheasant
2 wild duck
1 studded banana shallot or onion with cloves
10 green peppercorns
Bouquet garni
4 leaves of gelatine
4 celery sticks
1 carrot
Chopped parsley
Damson & Juniper Relish (see below)

Ingredients / Damson & Juniper Relish

450g damsons
45g brown sugar
10 crushed juniper berries
2 tsp cider vinegar
2 tbsp cider
4 sprigs of thyme

Method

Soak ham overnight in water. Drain water and place ham in water and bring to boil for 5 minutes, then drain and replace again with fresh water. Now add chopped celery, carrot, studded onion and bouquet garni.
Bring to the boil and simmer for 2-3 hours. Meanwhile dice pheasant breasts and duck breasts. Heat a non-stick pan and put in a knob of butter, then cook pheasant and duck pieces gently until pink. Place onto kitchen paper and drain. Drain ham and reduce remaining stock by half, soak gelatine in cold water to soften and add to stock and pass through a fine seive. Line terrine mould with 3 large lengths of cling film. Remove fat off ham, and shred it roughly when cool. Then mix with diced game and parsley. Press the meat down firmly into terrine mould and pour stock gently over the meat. Place in fridge overnight to set. Serve with relish.

Method / Damson & Juniper Relish

Place cider in a heavy pan, then add damsons, sugar and juniper berries. Cook for 5 minutes. Add cider vinegar and thyme, then cook for approximately 15 minutes. Place into food processor and blend until smooth. Put into jars.

'Robert the Gamekeeper'

Robert Crofts runs the Portavo Estate in Donaghadee and as such is a near neighbour of mine. Robert, who's originally from Suffolk, has been keepering all his working life. He's been at Portavo for twenty five years now, and is involved in all aspects of this small but very productive privately-owned estate.

A well-evolved in-house game rearing facility at Portavo means that they're able to oversee every stage in the rearing of game such as pheasant, partridge and duck (in fact, they're currently well along the road to receiving official accreditation from the Dept of Agriculture as an official game-handling establishment – a first for an estate in Northern Ireland). Robert's a man with a vast experience in his field, and has been Chairman of the British Association for Shooting and Conservation's Gamekeeper's Advisory Committee for the past two years.

According to what's in season, Robert supplies me regularly with home-cured burgers and sausages made from the game reared on the Estate, as well as fantastic oven-ready pheasants and partridges.

Products home-cured at Portavo have been a great success. Robert often recounts jokingly the time when, at the end of a shoot day on the Estate, one of the guest guns to whom he had just handed a pack of pheasant sausages was heard to remark gleefully: 'This really is a marvellous place. You shoot the birds in the morning, and by the time you leave, they've been made into sausages!'

Gravlax with Mustard Dressing

This recipe, dating back to the Middle Ages, is an interesting one. It was originally made by fishermen, by first salting the salmon and then burying the fish under the sand at the high tide line. Grav means to bury or hole in Scandinavian languages.

Serves 12

Ingredients / Gravlax

1 kg fresh Irish salmon
4 tbsp Maldon salt
4 tbsp caster sugar
2 tbsp cork dry gin
6 Juniper berries, crushed
Bunch of fresh dill
Mustard
Mustard dressing (see below)

Ingredients / Mustard Dressing

2 tbsp Dijon mustard
2 tsp caster sugar
1 egg yolk
150ml vegetable oil
1 tsp red wine vinegar
Chopped dill
1 tsp sloe gin

Method / Gravlax

Mix salt, sugar and crushed juniper berries in a bowl. Place salmon skin side down on a large tray, then splash gin over fish and cover with salt mix. Wrap in cling film and press in fridge for 48 hours. Brush off salt mix and rub with a dry clean cloth.Cover with mustard and fresh chopped dill and wrap again until set.With a sharp knife, slice salmon very thinly.Serve on a plate with a ramekin of mustard dressing, lemon and Guinness Wheaten Bread (see page 24).

Method / Mustard Dressing

Mix mustard, sugar and egg yolk over a bain-marie. Slowly add vinegar, oil and gin. Add chopped dill and season.

Mains

Luxury Fish Pie

This is a take on the famous Mrs Beeton's recipe.It's another great dish that I used to cook at the Clandeboye estate. Mrs Beeton was one of the first ever celebrity chefs.

Serves 4

Ingredients / Fish pie

455g coley or pollock fillets, skinned and cubed
115g mussel meat
55g scallops
115g langoustine or king tiger prawns
55g butter
55g plain flour
150ml dry white wine
425ml fish stock
1 bay leaf
1 fennel chopped
1 tsp fennel seeds
225ml double cream
1 tbsp parsley, chopped
1 tbsp fresh dill or fennel tops, chopped

Ingredients / Cheddar mash

8 large Desiree potatoes
100g butter, soft
50g grated cheddar cheese

Method / Fish pie

Preheat the oven to 220C. In a pot heat the butter, add the chopped fennel and fennel seeds, then the flour, stirring continuously. Add the wine and reduce, then add the stock, bay leaf and seasoning and pass through a fine seive. Add the fish, shellfish, cream and herbs. Pour into a 1.2 litre pie dish. Pipe cheddar mash on top of the fish sauce mixture. Bake for 20-25 minutes until golden brown.

Method / Cheddar mash

Peel potatoes and dice in even sizes, then place in a sauce pan with salted cold water and bring to boil. Gently cook until soft and tender. Drain potatoes into a colander then pass through a mouli or vegetable press sieve. Return pureed potatoes to a clean pot, add butter and cheese, and beat slowly until smooth. Season with white pepper and salt.

Five Hour Cooked Beef with Roasted Beetroot & Horseradish Mash

This dish has developed over the last few years into what it is today. We have used many different cuts of beef but we have now settled on the cut of beef called the Jacob's ladder/short rib. We use a great supplier called Kettyle Irish Beef. They are master butchers who really understand that the professional chef needs a great company selling local beef and rose veal.

Serves 4-6

Ingredients
2 kg short ribs
2 medium onions
2 cloves of garlic
2 celery sticks
1 carrot
330ml red wine
2 litres beef stock
Fresh thyme
6 black peppercorns
1 bay leaf

Ingredients / Roasted Beetroot
4 large beetroots
2 tbsp olive oil
2 tbsp red wine vinegar
Small bunch of thyme
2 tsp caster sugar

Ingredients / Horseradish Mash
900g Maris Piper potatoes
100 ml milk
3 tbsp creamed horseradish
Salt and white pepper

Method
Brown ribs on both sides, remove from casserole pot. In pot, reduce red wine by half.Add carrot, onion, celery and thyme to pot. Cover with beef stock and gently cook for 5 hours. Drain off stock and reduce until sauce thickens and pass through a fine sieve. Serve with beetroot and horseradish mash.

Method / Roasted Beetroot
Peel beetroot and cut into rounds with a pastry cutter and trim. Toss beetroot in oil and thyme. Roast on a tray in oven for 40-45 minutes at 190c, until soft. Sprinkle with caster sugar and vinegar and cook for a further 5 minutes.

Method / Horseradish Mash
Peel and dice potatoes into even sized chunks. Boil and simmer in salted water for 20 minutes until soft. Drain potatoes and return to pan for a few minute and dry. Pass potato through fine sieve or Mouli onto milk, then add horseradish and beat well with a spoon. Heat well and season.

Slow Braised Lamb Shanks with Saffron Crushed Potatoes & Roasted Peppers

A Grace Neill's old favourite from when I had the pub for many years. This is one of the cuts of lamb which I suppose was a signature dish – a true Irish gastropub dish. It is made with an inexpensive cut of lamb that is hearty and full of flavour, although I think the butchers have caught on to the popularity of this cut now and it's overpriced.

Serves 4

Ingredients / Lamb Shanks

4 lamb shanks
3 garlic cloves, crushed
4 sprigs fresh rosemary
3 tbsp olive oil
4 shallots, finely chopped
2 garlic cloves, finely sliced
250ml red wine
3 fresh tomatoes, roughly chopped
2 sprigs fresh rosemary
2 sprigs fresh thyme
750ml chicken or vegetable stock
Salt and freshly ground black pepper

Method / Lamb Shanks

Preheat the oven to 140C. To prepare the lamb, cut small incisions in each of the lamb shanks and firmly push herbs and garlic into the incisions. Heat a frying pan until hot and add one tablespoon of the olive oil to the pan. Add the lamb shanks and fry on each side for one minute until browned all over.

Meanwhile, add the remaining olive oil, shallots and garlic into a heated casserole dish and fry the shallots and garlic for about 2-3 minutes, until just softened, but not browned. Add the red wine and bring to the boil. Add the tomatoes, rosemary, thyme and return to the boil. Place the lamb shanks into the sauce and cover with the stock. Season with salt and freshly ground black pepper.

Bring to a simmer, cover and place in a really low heat oven to cook for at least 5 hours. The meat should be meltingly tender and ready to serve.

Ingredients / Crushed Saffron & Olive Oil Potatoes

1 kg Desiree potatoes, peeled and cut into chunks
Pinch of saffron
75ml olive oil
Salt and freshly ground black pepper

Ingredients / Roasted Red Peppers

4 red peppers
1 sprig of thyme & rosemary roughly chopped
2 tbsp of sherry vinegar
4 cloves of chopped garlic
Drizzle of extra virgin olive oil
Salt & pepper

Method / Crushed Saffron & Olive Oil Potatoes

Place the potatoes into a large saucepan and cover with water and saffron. Add a pinch of salt, place on the heat and bring to the boil. Simmer for 10-15 minutes until tender. Drain well and return to the pan over a low heat for a few seconds to remove any excess moisture. Using a potato masher, mash roughly, adding the olive oil to the potatoes. Season with salt and freshly ground black pepper.

Method / Roasted Red Peppers Method

Cut peppers in quarters keeping green stock on and deseed. Covers peppers with herbs, oil & garlic, and place under low grill for 15 minutes. Add sherry vinegar and seasoning and grill for a further 5 minutes.

Plating Up

To serve, remove the lamb shanks from the sauce and pass lamb sauce through a sieve. Reduce and season, always skimming fat off the sauce. Place lamb onto four serving plates. Place saffron potatoes on a plate, place peppers on top and then the lamb. Spoon the sauce over the lamb shanks, and spoon over a little extra olive oil to finish.

Wild Hake with Chickpea Puree & Prawn Chowder

Probably my favourite fish to cook. Funny that there is turbot and halibut, which are much more expensive fish, but I love this less expensive fish, the Silver Hake. When I think hake I think stew and, being an Ulster Scot, I then think potato, so that's where the chowder comes in. It's all about big robust flavours, and hake can stand up to these flavours. Chorizo sausage is also great with hake. Simply an outstanding fish.

Serves 4

Ingredients
4 x 225g hake

Ingredients / Poaching liquid
100ml white wine
1 1/5 litre fish stock
8 peppercorns
1 star anise
Parsley
Thyme
1 shallot, quartered

Ingredients / Chickpea puree
450g chickpeas, soaked overnight
2 cloves garlic
1 green chilli, chopped
150ml olive oil
Zest and juice of 1 lemon.

Method / Wild Hake
Place all poaching ingredients in a shallow pot/pan. Bring to a gentle boil, then simmer and place fish in and cover with buttered greaseproof paper and poach for 8-10 minutes.Lift out carefully and keep warm, drain fish stock and use for stock again.

Method / Chickpea puree
Drain and rinse chickpeas. Place into saucepan and cover with cold water, bring to boil and simmer for 45 minutes until soft. Don't add salt to the chick peas as it makes the shell turn tough.Drain and reserve 125ml of cooking liquid, place chickpeas, garlic, chilli, lemon and olive oil into food processor and blend until smooth. Add the remaining cooking liquid and season.

Ingredients / Prawn Chowder

1 tbsp olive oil
100g lean bacon, diced
1 large leek, white part only, finely sliced
Large pinch saffron
1 litre fish stock
1 bay leaf
2 large potatoes, peeled, halved and cut into small dice
330g tin sweetcorn kernels or 250g fresh corn kernels
500g peeled prawns
142ml double cream
Salt and freshly ground pepper

To finish

1 tbsp chopped parsley

Method / Poaching liquid

Heat the olive oil in a large saucepan over a medium heat, add the bacon and leek and fry gently for 10 minutes, without browning. Meanwhile, soak the saffron threads in hot water for a few minutes. Add the saffron to fish stock, bay leaf, bacon and leeks, and bring to the boil. Add the potatoes, return to the boil and simmer for 15 minutes, until the potatoes are soft but still keep their shape. Add the sweetcorn and the prawns to the chowder and cook until the prawns are just firm. Stir in the cream then remove from the heat. Adjust the seasoning and lift out the bay leaf.

Plating Up

Set the chickpea puree in the middle of a plate or pasta style bowl, set the hake on top, and pour chowder around.

Rump of Irish Lamb with Couscous Nicoise

I spent a short time working in my friend Michael Deane's restaurant and worked along side his great head chef Derek Creag. This is my interpretation of a dish I cooked with Derek.

Serves 4

Ingredients

250ml of vegetable stock
125g instant couscous or Orzo Pasta
Salt and pepper
50ml olive oil
1 small courgette
1/2 medium aubergine
1 red pepper
6 pitted black olives
50g butter
8 cloves garlic chopped
4 x 160g lamb rumps,
boned and trimmed

Ingredients / Sauce

150ml lamb jus
Finely chopped thyme
30g butter
Salt
Pepper

Method

Boil stock and add to couscous, cover and leave to rest. Season with salt and pepper and mix with one tablespoon of olive oil, stirring occasionally until cold. Put the rest of the oil in a pan, dice courgette, aubergine and red pepper into small dice and sweat in oil with garlic. Combine with the couscous and season, then add chopped olives.

Season meat and roast for 6-8 minutes in oven and then rest for a few minutes. Drain fat from pan, slightly heat lamb jus, finish with thyme, add butter, season and pass through a sieve. Place lamb on top of couscous and pour sauce around plate.

Wild Irish Venison & Roasted & Pureed Butternut Squash with Chocolate Sauce

When I spent time working in Clandeboye I gained a lot of respect for game and game keepers. It was only natural that I used game from the estate. Barry Garvin, the estates game keeper, would have kept me in supply of game when in season: rabbit, venison, wild duck, the odd guinea fowl, and of course, the estate's superb deer.

Serves 4

Ingredients / Venison
4 venison rumps or steaks/chops

Ingredients / Squash Puree
1/2 butternut squash (roughly diced)
50g butter
Zest of 1 orange
2 tsp maple syrup
Salt and pepper

Ingredients / Roast Squash
1/2 butternut squash (thick end)
1/2 tsp chilli flakes
Thyme
Olive oil
Knob of butter
Caster sugar

Ingredients / Chocolate Sauce
1 litre chicken stock
150ml red wine
2 tsp red wine vinegar
200g shallots, chopped
200g carrots
40g bitter chocolate, chopped
100g pancetta
Thyme
2 cloves of garlic, chopped

Method / Venison
Heat a heavy pan, add a little oil and cook venison until medium rare, about 1 ½ minutes on each side, and then leave to rest.

Method / Squash Puree
Simmer squash in salted water for 15 minutes until soft. Drain, then return to pan and steam for 1 minute, add zest, syrup and butter. Blend until smooth.

Method / Roast Squash
Dice squash into cubes, toss in oil, chilli, thyme and sugar. Put into hot pan, add butter and brown in oven for 5-7 minutes until just soft. Drain onto kitchen paper and keep warm.

Method / Chocolate Sauce
Sauté the onions, carrots and pancetta until golden brown. Add thyme, red wine and reduce by half. Pour stock in, bring to a gentle boil and simmer until reduced to a sauce consistency. Add grated chocolate and vinegar and simmer, then pass through a fine sieve.

Plating Up
Lay puree on plate and place roast squash around. Slice the warm venison and place onto puree & sauce with jus.

Beef & Oyster Pie

This dish is one I brought with me from my time at Grace Neills in Donaghadee. My vision for Grace Neills was to top quality traditional English pub style cooking, and bring it to the next level, offering dishes such as Dover sole with mussels, braised beef and Guinness hot pot, jellied eel and so on. It was 'gastropub' cuisine – long before that term was coined by food writers and journalists.

The combination of beef and oysters is a classic one in pub cooking, and I've given it my own spin here by serving it in a pie, which is presented in a beautiful copper pot. Diners always seem to appreciate the way the traditional theme of the dish is echoed in the presentation.

IN U.S.A.
ILHENNY
LA.
BAS

Beef & Oyster Pie

Another great, gutsy gastropub dish. My favourite oysters are from the beds of the Bob Graham's Dundrum Bay Oyster Fishery in County Down. They also sell fantastic large mussels which appear on the Jeffers menu as a special.

Serves 4

Ingredients

800g beef flank, cut into large cubes
250ml Belfast ale or Guinness Stout
1 tsp fresh thyme
30g butter
1 bay leaf
8 baby onions and shallots
1 tsp tomato puree
1 ½ pints beef stock
8 oysters
Chopped parsley
400g puff pastry
Salt and pepper
1 egg yolk

Method

Marinate beef in ale, thyme and bay leaf for 48 hours. Drain marinade off and reserve, then dry meat on kitchen roll. Melt butter in casserole pot, then add beef pieces and cook until brown. Add marinade and reduce by half, then add tomato puree and beef stock. Bring to boil and simmer, then place in oven for 2 1/2 hours until tender.

Allow mixture to cool and place into a pie dish, top with oysters and chopped parsley. Brush egg yolk around pie dish and top with puff pastry, brushing the pastry lid also with egg. Bake in oven at 200c for 20-30 minutes. Serving suggestion: Serve with glazed carrots or parsnips and Horseradish Mash (see page 88).

Baked Bream en Papillote with Peas a la Française

This is a great dish- a bit of theatre at the table. Your guests or family will love it.

Serves 4

Ingredients / Bream
4 small whole bream (deheaded), scored and gutted
1 fennel
1 small onion
4 tbsp butter
100ml white wine
Salt & pepper

Ingredients / Peas a la Francaise
50g butter
500g gem lettuce shredded
1 tsp parsley
1 tsp sugar
500g garden peas (fresh or frozen)
12 pickling onions
90ml chicken stock

Method / Bream
Brush fish on both sides with butter, place fish on a large piece of grease proof paper and add onion and fennel, splash with white wine, season and wrap. Cook for 10 minutes in a hot oven at 225c.

Method / Peas a la Francaise
Sauté pickling onions without colouring them, until soft. Add peas, lettuce, stock and sugar to pot and simmer gently for a few minutes. Finish with butter and parsley.

Plating up
Serve fish in the paper on a plate surround by peas. Cut parchment with scissors just prior to serving.

Irish Salmon with Dulse, Cucumber, Radish & Sprouts with Deep Fried Oysters

I suppose that the best salmon we have ever had on the market in Ireland was Glenarm Salmon, but unfortunately, they had a huge disaster with the jelly fish invasion in 2007. I'm glad to say they are back up and running again. This salmon recipe also works great with new season local lobster. The sweetness of the lobster really works well with the sharp and tart flavour of the dulse.

Serves 4

Ingredients
4 fillets of salmon
1 cucumber
1 bag red radish
1 bag dulse
4 rock oysters
1 punnet of cress or micro sprouts
Fish stock

Ingredients / Ponzo Dressing
250ml soy sauce
125ml mirin
60ml white wine
1/4 red chilli (diced)
Chives
Coriander

Ingredients / Deep Fried Oyster
4 oysters (keep juice for dressing)
2 beaten eggs
Breadcrumbs
Flour

Method
Gently poach salmon in fish stock for 5 minutes or grill for 1 ½ minutes on each side. Peel cucumber, de-seed and cut into fine strips. Slice red radish very thinly Cut sprouts with scissors. Finely cut dulse.

Method / Ponzo Dressing
Bring soy, mirin and wine to the boil and reduce by half. Cool, then add chilli and chopped fresh herbs. Add oyster juice.

Method / Deep Fried Oyster
Flour, egg and breadcrumb oysters twice. Deep fry at 180c, drain onto kitchen paper.

Smoked Fish Cakes with Lobster Mayonnaise & Tomato Relish

You can use coley or pollock, which are of the cod family, half the price of cod and not overfished. This fish can be deep fried, grilled, baked, and poached, and we also get them at Jeffers smoked by our fish supplier. Keep asking your local fishmonger and I'm sure they will be able to source them for you, but let's keep them out of the supermarkets.

Serves 4

Ingredients

750g natural smoked pollock, coley, haddock or cod.
750g new potatoes peeled
50g butter
Chopped parsley
Salt and pepper
2 beaten eggs
100g flour
100g breadcrumbs (super fine)

Ingredients / Lobster Mayonnaise

2 free-range egg yolks
1 tsp Dijon mustard
150ml olive oil
150ml vegetable oil
Squeeze lemon juice
Salt and pepper
1 lobster claw meat
Parsley
4 gherkins chopped
1 drop green Tabasco

Method

Gently steam fish over hot water, covered for 15-20 minutes. Cook potatoes in salted water until soft. Drain and return to pan and steam for a further 2 minutes. Crush potatoes, add fish when slightly cooled, then add parsley and season. Form into fish cakes-flour, egg wash and breadcrumb twice. Deep fry in oil for 7 minutes until crisp and golden.

Method / Lobster Mayonnaise

Put egg yolks, mustard and salt into a food processor. Blend until smooth, start turning slowly, speed up and add oils slowly until thick. Put into bowl and add chopped lobster, parsley and gherkins.

Ingredients / Tomato relish

1 shallot finely sliced
1 clove garlic crushed
800g tin of chopped tomatoes
1 red chilli chopped finely
200ml sherry vinegar
100g sugar
2 tbsp maple syrup
Salt and pepper
Basil, finely chopped.

Method / Tomato relish

Fry shallot, garlic and chilli until soft. Add tomatoes and cook well for 10 minutes. Add vinegar and sugar and bring to boil and simmer for 15-20 minutes until thick.Season with salt and pepper and add basil.

Free Range Chicken Breast & Black Pudding

Lots of countries claim they invented black pudding (aka blood sausage), from the North of England, to Scotland, Ireland, France and even Poland. There are many takes on the sausage but my personal favourite is a northern version by O'Dohertys of Enniskillen. They also sell outstanding real black bacon. If you are ever in Enniskillen it's a must.

Serves 4

Ingredients

2 tbsp oil
50g butter
2 shallots, chopped
175g black pudding, crumbled
2 tbsp chopped thyme
Black pepper
4 free range chicken breast fillets
8 slices of streaky bacon

Ingredients / Pearl Barley Chicken Jus

6 shallots
100ml port
250ml red wine
1 litre of brown chicken stock
Salt and pepper
Cooked pearl barley

Method

Heat 1 tablespoon of oil and 25g of butter in a heavy-based frying pan. Add the chopped shallots and the black pudding and fry, stirring, for 3-5 minutes. Season with salt and freshly ground pepper, mix in thyme and drain and set aside to cool. Preheat the oven to 190°C. Using a sharp knife, cut a pocket in the thick side of each chicken breast fillet. Fill each pouch with the cooled black pudding mixture. Wrap each chicken breast fillet in 2 slices of streaky bacon.

Heat 1 tablespoon of olive oil and 25g of butter in a large, heavy-based frying pan. Add in the bacon wrapped chicken breasts and fry until coloured on each side, around five minutes. Transfer the chicken breasts to a roasting tray and roast in the oven for 5-8 minutes. Serve with pearl barley, chicken jus and seasonal vegetables.

Method / Pearl Barley Chicken Jus

Place slice shallots into a heavy pan and add port and red wine and reduce to a glaze. Add the chicken stock and bring to a boil, skimming off the scum. Simmer and reduce until a sauce consistency. Pass through a sieve, add cooked barley and season.

Roast Saddle of Monkfish with Samphire, Tomato, Cockle & Saffron

The popularity of monkfish has exploded in the last 20 years. Fishermen tell me that monkfish would have been used as bait in years gone by, as it's such an ugly fish, yet it's so firm and meaty in flavour. The cheeks are also very fashionable on many menus these days. I also love fish on the bone. It really helps the flavour and is also good for barbecuing. Try it wrapped with good quality streaky bacon.

Serves 4

Ingredients / Monkfish
4 small monkfish on the bone

Ingredients / Samphire
150g samphire
Pepper
Knob of butter
Lemon juice

Ingredients / Tomato
2 large tomatoes

Ingredients / Sauce
100ml dry white wine
1 shallot thinly sliced
2 garlic cloves, chopped
Thyme
Parsley
1kg cockles, scrubbed
750ml fish stock
Pinch of saffron
400ml double cream

Method / Monkfish
Saute monkfish in heavy pan with olive oil, and place in oven at 220c for 10-12 minutes until cooked.

Method / Samphire
Bring a pot of water to a boil, place in samphire for 2-3 minutes. Drain then toss in butter and lemon juice. Season with black pepper.

Method / Tomato
Boil a kettle of water. Score tomatoes and place into a bowl and pour over boiling water. Leave for about 40-60 seconds. Put into ice water and peel, deseed and dice.

Method / Sauce

Heat butter in saucepan over high heat, add shallot and garlic and cook until soft. Add pinch of saffron and thyme, then add wine and reduce by half. Add stock and cream and bring to the boil and simmer for 5 minutes. Pass through a fine sieve into a container and then return to pot. Cook cockles with lid on until open and finish with parsley and diced tomatoes.

Plating Up

Place samphire in large type pasta bowl, then monkfish and pour sauce all around to finish.

Crisp Duck Confit with Red Cabbage & Cider Braised Potatoes

Confit, from the French verb confire, which means to preserve. It is said that this was the one of the very first ways to preserve meat. Still a very popular dish in many restaurants across the globe, this is a timeless recipe.

Serves 4

Ingredients

4 large male duck legs, jointed and trimmed
3 heaped tsp Maldon salt
Thyme sprigs
1 tsp five spice powder
4 cloves garlic
Goose fat

Ingredients / Red Cabbage

1 small red cabbage
50g salt
250g sherry vinegar
400ml red wine
2 star anise
1 cinnamon stick
6 cloves
10 juniper berries, crushed
1 tsp green peppercorns
125g caster sugar

Ingredients / Cider Braised Potatoes

1 kg Maris Piper potatoes, thinly sliced
1 ½ litres chicken stock
½ litre cider
50g butter
Sprig of thyme

Method

Marinate duck in salt, thyme, spice and crushed garlic. Cover and keep in fridge for 24 hours. Brush off marinade and gently braise and cover in goose fat for 1 ½ - 2 hours. Take out of goose fat and crisp under a grill before serving.

Method / Red Cabbage

Shred cabbage finely and place into heavy deep pot. Sprinkle with salt and leave for 2 hours. Wash off salt and dry. Add vinegar, wine and sugar to cabbage, bring to boil and reduce by half, which should take about an hour. Blend all spices in a food processor and then add to cabbage and reduce for 10 minutes, letting the spices infuse.

Method / Cider Braised Potatoes

Set oven to 200c. Bring stock, cider and butter to the boil and reduce by half.
Layer potatoes in an oven proof dish and pour over stock liquid, then sprinkle with thyme. Brush top layer with melted butter and cook for 45 minutes until soft.
Push skewer through potatoes, if not soft cook for a further few minutes.

Five Spiced Pork Belly with Parsnips & Apple

A great cut of meat which I believe did not appear on many restaurant menus for years because of snobbery. As you can see in the picture of this dish on page 60, we have a selection of cuts of pork on one plate. We call this a plate of Irish pork and it's a great tasting plate. There is a little farm shop in Comber called Pheasant Hill where they sell great pork.

Serves 4-6

Ingredients

900g pork belly
7 or 5 spice powder
4 sticks celery
1 carrot
1 leek
2 bay leaves
500ml chicken stock
125ml cider

Ingredients / Maple roasted baby parsnips

650g baby parsnips or 8 large parsnips
40g butter
3/4 tsp maple syrup
Salt and ground black pepper

Ingredients / Parsnip Cream

400g diced parsnip
20g butter
35 ml cream
25 ml milk
Pinch of caster sugar
Salt

Method

Rub pork belly with spice and cover for 16 hours. Roughly chop vegetables and brown in a pan. Place vegetables in a deep roasting tray and lace pork on top. Cover with stock and cider. Place in oven and cook on very low heat for 3-4 hours. Remove meat from tray carefully and sieve stock into sauce pan and reduce by half until reaches a sauce consistency. Cut pork into portions and grill until crisp.

Method / Maple roasted baby parsnips

Peel and split parsnip in half. Butter a roasting tray and set oven at 180c. Toss parsnip in maple syrup in and season Cook for 20 minutes until just soft.

Method / Parsnip Cream

Place parsnips in heavy pan with butter, milk, salt and caster sugar. Cook parsnips until soft, this should take about 20 minutes. Place in food processor, add cream and whizz until smooth.

Ingredients / Apple Puree

6 Granny smith apples, peeled, cored and cubed.
60g butter
Juice of 2 lemons
125g Caster sugar

Method / Apple Puree

Cook apples in butter and sugar until soft.
Add lemon and reduce until soft, then puree in food processor until smooth. Keep warm.

Plating Up

Place parsnip cream on plate and lay parsnips around plate.
Crisp pork under grill and set on plate and top with reduced pork sauce, and serve apple puree separately.

Steak & Chips

Irish beef is, in my opinion, the best in the world. By far my favourite cut is the ribeye. When I owned Grace Neill's, this was by far the best selling dish on the menu for years. It's the simplicity of this dish that people love. True flavours, no big sauces overpowering the sublime taste of the beef, and perfect chips are all you need. If you prefer a sauce with your steak, I have included an option for a garlic Béarnaise sauce. Of course, serve medium rare.

Serves 4

Ingredients / Chips
4 large Desiree or Maris Piper potatoes
Salt and freshly ground black pepper

Ingredients / Steak
4 ribeye steaks
(approx 200g-250g each)
Salt and freshly ground black pepper
2 tbsp oil
25g butter

Ingredients / Garlic Béarnaise Sauce
1 shallot, finely chopped
1 tsp of chopped garlic
1 tsp tarragon leaves
4 tbsp dry white wine
2 tbsp white wine vinegar
175g unsalted butter
3 egg yolks, at room temperature

Method / Steak
To make the chips: preheat fryer to 120c. Fill a large pan with boiling water, add a pinch of salt and place over a high heat. Cut each potato into chips. Add the chips to the boiling water, bring to the boil again and boil for 3 minutes. Drain in a colander and then place the colander sitting over the pan. Tip the chips into the fryer basket and blanch for a few minutes, then lift basket and turn fryer up to 180c. To cook the steak: place a large frying pan over a high heat and leave until smoking hot. Place the steaks onto a large chopping board and season the steaks on both sides with salt and black pepper. Once the frying pans have reached maximum temperature, add approximately two tablespoons of oil. Carefully lay the steaks in the hot frying pan. Tilt the pan away from you so that the fat is touching the side of the pan to ensure the fat is cooked and golden. Shake the pan to make sure the steaks aren't sticking. Fry for 1½ minutes and then add the butter to the pan. Spoon the melted butter on each side of the steaks to baste them. Remove the steaks from the pan and set aside to rest.

Method / **Garlic Béarnaise Sauce**

Put the shallot, garlic, tarragon, 4 tbsp water, and white wine vinegar in a small pan. Boil for 2–3 minutes to reduce by a third. Once strained, you should have about 3 tbsp. Cool slightly. Melt the butter in a pan over a slow heat, until foaming. Continue to cook for 1 minute, or until the foam turns, and skim this and discard. Allow the butter to cool slightly. Mix the egg yolks and reduction in a blender, or use a hand-held blender. Slowly add the butter in a thin, steady stream, whisking until a light sauce forms. Season with salt and white pepper. And add chopped taragon. Fry chips at 180c and serve with steak and garlic Béarnaise suace.

Lobster with Tartare Hollandaise & Chips

If you happened to be in Bangor over the summer months, and in lobster season, call into Jeffers any Thursday night and you'll find our local harbour's lobster's catch on offer, usually served Thermidor-American or as a Lobster salad. What a treat– not to be missed!

Serves 4

Ingredients / Lobster

2-4 whole live lobsters, 1.8kg each
3 litres water
1 stick of celery
1 small bulb of fennel
1 shallot, chopped
2 bay leaves
6 peppercorns.

Ingredients / Tartare Hollandaise

Hollandaise sauce (see page 28)
1 tsp capers
1 tsp gherkins
1 tsp parsley
1 tsp tarragon
1 hard boiled egg, sieved.

Method / Lobster

In a large pot place water, celery, fennel, bay leaves, shallots and peppercorns and bring to boil. Put lobster in liquid and boil for ten minutes, then place into ice cold water and split into two.

Method / Tartare Hollandaise

Mix all ingredients with hollandaise in bowl. Place over split lobster and grill for 3-5 minutes. Serve with chips (see page 90), lemon and watercress.

Desserts

White Chocolate Raspberry Cheesecake

White chocolate and raspberries are a great marriage. I love this cheesecake, as either the baked type or gelantine set style of cheesecake both work great. When on the menu at Jeffers we serve this with Tim Morrow's fantastic raspberry sorbet, which you can purchase on his Streamvale farm in Dundonald, which is also a great day out for the kids.

Serves 8-12

Ingredients

210g biscuit crumbs
2 tbsp butter, melted
950g cream cheese, softened
250g sugar
3 large eggs
240ml double cream
1 tsp vanilla extract or vanilla seeds
180g white chocolate, chopped, melted and allowed to cool slightly
80ml fresh raspberries

To serve

Whipping cream
Fresh raspberries
Mint sprigs

Method

Crush the biscuits finely then combine in a bowl with the butter. Stir thoroughly to combine, then press into the base of a 22cm diameter springform cake tin or small one portion moulds. Beat cream cheese until smooth, then add the sugar and beat until thoroughly blended. Now add the eggs, one at a time, beating thoroughly to combine after each addition. Whisk in the cream and vanilla extract. Add the raspberries and melted chocolate to cream cheese mix and add chopped chocolate. Transfer to an oven pre-heated to 160°C and bake for about 80 minutes. Remove from the oven and allow to cool completely before removing from tins.Garnish with raspberry puree, raspberries and fresh mint leaves before serving.

Chocolate Guinness Brownies

Ahh the Guinness and chocolate brownie, which really should have been called the Jeffers brownie anyway. I remember coming up with this recipe in the old days with a young chef who works with me called David Mooney. It's one I developed during my 'gastropub' days at Grace Neill's, and so some sort of alcohol was always going to be a vital ingredient. To give the brownies that 'boozy twist' we tried all sorts of whiskey and Cointreau as well, but in the end, we came back to good old Guinness as the magic ingredient. The malt and chocolate flavours marry together perfectly, and the back stuff gives a rich moistness to the recipe which makes it really special. It got such good reviews it ended up in a book called *The New Irish Table*.

This is the recipe that was featured on Martha Stewart's very popular US television shows, as I mentioned at the beginning of this book.

Serves 8 to 10

Ingredients

4 eggs
85g caster sugar
250g bittersweet chocolate, chopped
125g white chocolate, chopped
6 tbsp unsalted butter
125g all-purpose flour
125g cocoa powder
285ml Guinness Stout

Method

Preheat the oven to 375° F. Butter an 8-inch-square pan. In an electric mixer, combine the eggs and sugar. Beat until light and fluffy. In a medium saucepan over medium heat, melt the bittersweet chocolate and butter, stirring until smooth. Remove from heat and beat into the egg mixture. Sift the flour and cocoa together and beat into the chocolate mixture and add white chocolate. Whisk in the Guinness. Pour into the pan and bake for 20 to 25 minutes, or until a skewer inserted in the centre comes out almost clean. Remove from the oven and let cool on a wire rack. To serve, dust the brownies with icing sugar and cut into squares.

monday CLOSED
sunday 11

Apple & Vanilla Panna Cotta with Granola Biscuits

This is a great way to use Lindy Guinness's yoghurt from her award winning herd at Clandeboye. I also use their granola for the biscuits. I came up with the idea while buying the yoghurt at the dairy farmshop at Clandeboye. Sometimes ideas just come to you that way. I guess I never switch off from cooking.

Serves 4-6

Ingredients / Panna Cotta

3 gelatine leaves
125ml milk
125ml Clandeboye yoghurt
255ml cream
1 vanilla pod, split lengthways and seeds scraped out.
30g sugar
60g apple puree

Ingredients / Biscuits

225g flour
175g butter
100g caster sugar
125g granola
2 eggs
2 egg yolks
Vanilla Sugar (see page 20)

Method / Panna Cotta

Soak gelatine in cold water. Place the cream, milk, yoghurt, sugar, vanilla pod and scraped seeds into a pan and simmer. Squeeze water out of gelatine, add to milk mixture, take off heat and dissolve gelatine. Add the apple puree. Pass through a sieve and divide the mixture between four and six ramekins and leave to cool. Place in fridge for at least 1 hour until set.

Method / Biscuits

Cream butter and sugar until fluffy. Slowly add eggs and yolks. Fold in flour and granola. Roll out and cut into pieces. Cook in medium oven for approximately 15 mins. Leave biscuits to cool and sprinkle with vanilla sugar. Turn Panna Cotta out onto a plate or leave in ramekins and serve with biscuits.

Pear & Blackberry Crumble (see photo on page 94)

This is a great autumn dish. I love late September when blackberries are just ready. They are plentiful around where I live so when I have a spare hour away from the restaurant, my kids and I will head around the lake behind our house and pick the most amazing wild blackberries.

Serves 4-6

Ingredients

6 large pears
30g butter
150g caster sugar
Pinch of cinnamon
80g frozen or fresh blackberries

Ingredients / Topping

50g sugar
50g butter diced
110g plain flour
50g oats or granola

Method

Peel and core pears and cut into 6 pieces. Heat butter in pan with sugar & cinnamon, add pears until soft. Add blackberries and put into pie dish. Put all topping ingredients into food processor and blitz until breadcrumb stage. Sprinkle over fruit and cook until golden brown (approximately 15-20 minutes). Serve with vanilla ice cream or custard.

Passion Fruit Posset & Sable Biscuits

A tip – when making posset don't overheat the cream, and let the cream cool slightly or the posset won't set correctly.

Serves 4-6

Ingredients / Passion Fruit Posset
850ml double cream
255g caster sugar
Juice and zest of 3 lemons
Pulp of 3 passion fruits

Ingredients / Sable Biscuits
225g flour
175g butter
100g caster sugar
1 egg
Egg yolks
Zest of 1 lemon
1 tsp poppy seeds

Method / Passion Fruit Posset
Bring cream, sugar and zest slowly to just under a boil. Simmer for a minute.
Allow to cool. Add lemon juice and passion fruit pulp and mix gently. Place into glasses. Allow to set.

Method / Sable Biscuits
Cream butter and sugar until fluffy. Slowly add egg and yolk. Fold in flour, poppy seeds and zest. Chill in fridge for 1 hour. Bind together and roll out and cut out into preferred shapes. Cook at 180C for approx 10 mins.

Garnish with fresh raspberries or passion fruit.

Poached Pears with Chocolate Sauce

This old classic is timeless. Try stuffing the pear when poached with crushed amaretti biscuits and add a splash of amaretto in your chocolate sauce. Big flavours!

Serves 4

Ingredients / Poached Pears

4 ripe firm pears, such as Bosc, Bartlett or D'Anjou
235ml of apple juice or pear juice
175ml maple syrup
2 star anise, slightly crushed
1 1/2 teaspoons Thyme Leaves
4 strips lemon peel

Ingredients / Chocolate Sauce

200g plain chocolate,
50% cocoa solids, chopped
2 tbsp golden syrup
142ml double cream
1 grated zest and juice of a small orange

Method / Poached Pears

Peel and core pears from the bottom, leaving stems intact. Cut a thin slice off the bottom of each pear to provide a flat surface, and core the inside with a Parisienne scoop. Put into water with slice of lemon and set aside. Mix remaining ingredients in large saucepan. Bring to boil. Place pears in liquid in saucepan, standing pears with stems pointing up. Reduce heat to low; simmer, covered, 20 to 30 minutes or until pears are tender. Leaves pears in the saucepan and cool. Serve with chocolate sauce.

Method / Chocolate Sauce

Prepare a water bath no more than one-third full. Rest pan or bowl over the bath just touching the water, and add the chocolate, zest, orange juice, golden syrup and cream into the pan or bowl. Heat gently until everything in the pan or bowl has melted, then stir to combine. Keep the sauce warm and runny until you are ready to serve

Star Anise Creme Brulee with Lychees

I wonder how many other people remember getting tinned fruit with cold custard as a staple childhood or teenage dessert. My mother used to serve it up to us on a regular basis at home, and it was a great 'school dinner' classic in those days too. Although it was cheap and cheerful in terms of ingredients, it was tasty and comforting too, and one of my own favourites. This is a modern spin on it – taken up a few notches. The anise seed and ginger add a touch of the exotic. A great dessert for the winter months.

Serves 4

Ingredients / Creme Brulee

175g caster sugar
9 egg yolks
4 star anise
100ml milk
900ml cream
Brown sugar
Fresh / Tinned Lychees

Method / Creme Brulee

Pre-heat oven to 120c. Mix the sugar and yolks in a bowl until cream colour. Add star anise to milk and cream. Bring the milk and cream mixture slowly to the boil. Take out the star anise. Pour onto sugar/egg yolk mix, stirring at the same time. Pour the brulee mixture into 8 ramekins, not too full.
Put the ramekins into a bain-marie and cook in low oven for approximately 30-40 minutes or until they are set with just a slight wobble in the middle. When cooled, sprinkle each brulee with a good dusting of sugar and blow torch until a golden brown, leave to cool again before serving.

Serve with tinned lychees and ginger shortbread (see page 108)

Lime Tart

This is my take on lemon tart, the signature dish of Marco Pierre White, a true genius – the Godfather.

Serves 8 - 12

Ingredients / Pastry
500g plain flour
175g icing sugar
Grated zest of 1 lime
Seeds of vanilla
1 1/2 eggs

Ingredients / Filling
9 eggs
400g caster sugar
10 limes and zest of 2 more
250 ml double cream

Method / Pastry
Mix flour, lime zest and vanilla. Work in butter to flour mix until breadcrumb stage Beat eggs in well, knead mixture well and set in fridge for half hour. Now roll in flan ring, line with baking beans. Bake at180c for 15-20mins and leave to cool.

Method / Filling
Whisk eggs, zest and sugar together. Stir in lime juice and fold in cream. Remove any froth before filling tart case.

Baking tart
Set oven to 120c. Pour cold filling into tart case. Bake for 30 minutes until set. Leave to cool and then slice and serve with fresh raspberries and raspberry sorbet.

Poached Rhubarb & Ginger Shortbread

I love rhubarb when in season and it's great served either hot or cold.

Serves 4

Ingredients / Shortbread

200g unsalted butter
100g caster sugar
1 egg yolk
250g plain flour, plus extra for dusting
Pinch of powder ginger
Icing sugar, for dusting

Ingredients / Rhubarb

6 stalks rhubarb
50g caster sugar
20ml cranberry juice

Ingredients / Sabayon Sauce

50g caster sugar
50 ml water
1egg yolks
50ml dessert wine

Method / Shortbread

Cream the butter and sugar together in a round-bottomed bowl until light and fluffy. Add the egg yolk and mix in lightly. Add the flour, ginger powder and use your fingers to rub it in, creating a crumb texture. Knead the mixture to form a smooth dough. Wrap in cling film and leave to rest for 1 hour. On a floured work surface, roll out the dough to about 3mm thick. Cut into rectangles measuring 7.5 x 2cm, place on a non-stick baking tray and leave to rest in the fridge for approximately 10 minutes. Preheat the oven to 170C/gas 3. Bake the shortbread until it is a light sand colour - too much browning will result in a bitter taste. Set aside to cool.

Method / Rhubarb

Cut rhubarb into 7.5 x 2 cm batons. Place in a saucepan with the sugar and cranberry juice and poach gently for 3 - 5 minutes until the rhubarb is tender. Remove the rhubarb with a slotted spoon and cool. Bring the cooking liquid to a boil and simmer until it has reduced to a glaze consistency and cool.

Method / Sabayon sauce

Combine the caster sugar and water in a saucepan. Stir over a low heat until the sugar dissolves, then bring to a boil and simmer for 2-3 minutes to create a light syrup, then set aside to cool. Fill a medium saucepan with 3-5 cm of water and bring to a low simmer. Combine the sugar syrup, egg yolks and wine in a large heatproof bowl and place over the pan of steaming water. Whisk together until the mixture starts to foam, then continue cooking, gently whisking constantly, until the sauce is cooked, light and fluffy.

Plating Up

To serve, put rhubarb into the glaze. Lay one piece of shortbread on top rhubarb. Spoon over some of the sabayon. Repeat the process, then top with a piece of shortbread, dusted with icing sugar. Drizzle the rhubarb glaze around the outside of the plate.

Champagne Sorbet

Up until the last two years of poor local strawberry seasons, I would have used strawberries from Ballywalter estate, where you can also pick your own berries when they are in season. It's a great family day out. Let's hope next year brings a better yield there.

Serves 4

Ingredients / Sorbet

Juice and zest of 1 lemon
200ml water
175g sugar
1 tbsp liquid glucose
250ml champagne, cava or prosecco

Ingredients / Champagne Jelly

225g strawberries
Juice of 1 lemon
80g caster sugar
4 sheets of leaf gelatine
1 ½ bottles of champagne, Cava or Prosecco
100g Fraises des Bois (wild strawberries liquor), plus extra to decorate

Method / Sorbet

Place the lemon juice, water, sugar and liquid glucose in a small saucepan. Stir well, then heat gently until the sugar dissolves. Bring the pan to the boil, then remove from the heat and allow to cool to room temperature. Add the champagne- a good quality Cava or Prosecco works well- and transfer to an electric ice-cream maker. Churn for 30 minutes and serve immediately with the champagne jelly.

Method / Champagne Jelly

Hull and quarter the strawberries and place in a bowl set over a pan of gently simmering water. Stir in the lemon juice and sugar. Cover the bowl with clingfilm (or pan lid) and leave to steam for 20 minutes until the strawberries have softened and released their juices. Soak the gelatine sheets in a bowl of cold water to soften. Pick up the gelatine sheets and squeeze out the excess water. Bring sugar and champagne to a gentle boil. Mix in gelantine with champagne or sparkling wine and leave to cool completely. Meanwhile, add Fraises des Bois and divide between 4 glasses . Whisk the jelly until frothy and pour over the strawberries, which will float to the top. Chill for a few hours or overnight until set. Serve with the champagne sorbet.

Index